# GENESIS

## FROM CREATION TO THE FLOOD

CAMPFIRE®

KALYANI NAVYUG MEDIA PVT LTD

# GENESIS
## FROM CREATION TO THE FLOOD

Adapted by: Jason Quinn

Illustrated by: Naresh Kumar

Colorist: Vijay Sharma

Editors: Jason Quinn, Sourav Dutta

Design: Era Chawla

Lettering: Bhavnath Chaudhary

CAMPFIRE®

**Mission Statement**

To entertain and educate young minds by creating unique illustrated books that recount stories of human values, arouse curiosity in the world around us, and inspire with tales of great deeds of unforgettable people.

Published by Kalyani Navyug Media Pvt Ltd
101 C, Shiv House, Hari Nagar Ashram,
New Delhi 110014, India

ISBN: 978-93-81182-03-1

## CREATION

In the beginning *God* created the heaven and the earth.

And the earth was without form. And the spirit of *God* moved upon the face of the waters.

LET THERE BE LIGHT!

And *God* called the light Day, and the darkness he called Night.

There was evening and there was morning. This was the first day.

On the second day, God created a dome to separate the waters from the earth from the waters above.

And *God* named the dome Heaven.

And God said, 'Let the waters under the heaven be gathered together, and let the dry land appear.'

And God called the dry land Earth and the gathering together of the waters he called Seas.

And God said, 'Let the earth bring forth grass and plants and fruit bearing trees with seeds.'

This was the third day.

And on the fourth day God said, 'Let there be lights in the heavens to divide the day from the night.'

And God made two great lights, the greater light to rule the day and the lesser light to rule the night.

And on the fifth day God said 'Let the waters teem with life.' And he created the whales and the fish and the creatures of the sea.

And God said 'Let the birds fly up into the heavens.' And he created the winged birds to fill the skies.

And on the sixth day God created the beasts and the wildlife and the creeping things.

And *God* made man in his image.

And *God* breathed life into man.

And *God* named the man Adam.

...and He named the woman Eve.

And on the seventh day God ended His work and rested.

The Lord God planted a beautiful garden to the East for Adam and Eve to live in.

And in this fertile land grew every tree that is pleasant to the sight and good for food.

And in the middle of this garden grew the tree of knowledge of good and evil.

EAT FREELY FROM EVERY TREE IN THIS GARDEN... BUT NEVER TOUCH THE FRUIT OF THE TREE OF KNOWLEDGE OF GOOD AND EVIL.

FOR THE DAY YOU EAT ITS FRUIT WILL BE THE DAY THAT YOU SURELY DIE!

It was an idyllic life.

Ha! Eve! Look what I caught!

Unhappiness did not exist in the world.

You're such a beauty, aren't you?

And yet, something was not quite right...

How can something that looks so good be so bad?

?

>ahem<

Who are you?

A friend. Your husband, Adam callsss me the ssserpent.

Beautiful, isssn't it?

Ssshall we tasssste it?

No! Don't!

SNAP!

oh!

15

Mmmm!

CRUNCH!

It's delicious. It's...

...Eve! You... you're naked! Have you no shame?

And their eyes were truly opened and for the first time, Adam and Eve felt shame in their nakedness.

Me? What about you?

Stop staring at me!

And for their crime, Adam and Eve were cast out of Paradise, clothed in the skins of animals and forced to till the earth for their food.

And to prevent them from eating the fruit of the tree of life a flaming sword was set up along with a guard of Cherubims.

LEAVE THIS PLACE AND DO NOT RETURN!

The family were happy and Cain and Abel were constant companions...

Come Abel, I'll race you to the top of the tree!

But... wait for me.

Ha, Cain! See you at the top!

Hey!

Come on, Cain! I thought this was supposed to be a race.

Little show-off.

The years passed and Cain and Abel grew up strong and tall. Cain became a farmer, a tiller of the ground.

>Nnngh< Come on!

It was a hard life, full of toil and not without danger.

HISSS!

THUNK!

Huh?

While Cain farmed the land, Abel became a shepherd.

The family were close, living together, eating together and praying together...

We thank you, oh Lord for this bounteous feast.

I want to show God how much I love him. I would like to give him a present... An offering...

What an idiot. As if God would be interested in anything he has to offer.

I think that is a wonderful idea, Abel. Cain, you should prepare something to offer the Lord too.

Huh?

I'm going to make a beautiful altar to put my offering on too. It has to look just perfect.

Come on, Cain. There's no time to eat. Let's prepare our offerings for the Lord.

He's right, son. You can eat later.

Fine! I'm coming.

This is ridiculous. Why can't we do this after dinner?

44

45

Have mercy. You are driving me out. You are hiding your face from me.

How can I live without you? Everyone that finds me will try to slay me for what I have done. Everyone will hate me.

NO. FOR WHOEVER SLAYS CAIN, MY VENGEANCE WILL FALL UPON HIM SEVEN-FOLD.

I WILL SET MY MARK UPON YOU, AS A WARNING TO OTHERS NOT TO SLAY YOU.

ARRRGGH!

SSSSSSSSS!

NOW GO! LEAVE THIS PLACE!

And so the first murderer was banished...

I am so sorry, Abel. I'm so sorry, Mother. I am so sorry, Father.

Adam and Eve were heartbroken. Thanks to Cain's act of madness they had lost not one son, but two.

My boys... my beautiful boys...

Shhh. Be strong.

What is to become of us? I miss my boys so much.

We will be strong and we will endure.

And in time, Eve gave birth to another son, and called him Seth.

God is good. And so is Seth.

We are truly blessed.

And Seth grew strong and in time he too had children. And the race of man prospered.

And cities grew and years passed and men began to call upon the name of the Lord and worship him.

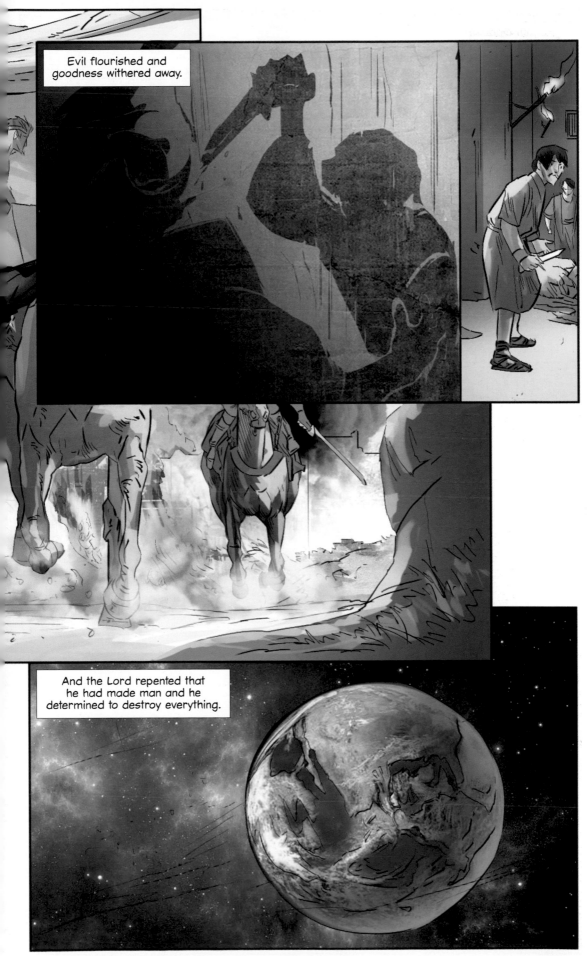

Evil flourished and goodness withered away.

And the Lord repented that he had made man and he determined to destroy everything.

But God noticed one of the descendants of Adam and Eve's son, Seth, and his name was Noah. He and his family were good people.

Let us first give praise to the Lord for the food which we are about to eat.

And the Lord decided to speak with Noah...

BE NOT AFRAID, NOAH, FOR IT IS I THE LORD AND I AM PLEASED WITH YOU.

What is this?

THE TIME IS NIGH FOR ALL FLESH TO DIE; FOR THE EARTH IS FILLED WITH VIOLENCE. I WILL DESTROY THEM ALL AND MAKE THE EARTH CLEAN.

PREPARE AN ARK OF GOPHER WOOD AND USE PITCH TO SEAL IT BOTH WITHIN AND WITHOUT.

At last, the animals were led two by two into the ark.

And then, just seven days later...

Hey, look, it's raining!

Noah must be happy!

HA! HA! HA

The rain began to fall, heavier and heavier...

I'm getting soaked. Run for it!

Maybe Noah was right.

Don't be ridiculous. It's just a shower.

The waters began to rise...

...and rise...

...and rise.

Batten down the hatches! Cast off the gangplank!

The waters crept higher, washing away the gangplank to the ark.

AYYEEE!

Whole towns and cities were destroyed.

WHOOOSH!

And still the rains fell.

But inside the ark, all were safe.

Everything we knew has perished. Everything we loved is lost.

Not everything, mother...

And the waters prevailed upon the earth for one hundred and fifty days.

When will this rain stop?

In the Lord's own good time.

Father, we can't hold out forever. Our supplies are running low.

We can last one month maybe two, but no longer.

The Lord will see us through these troubled times.

Oh, Lord, remember us in our time of trouble.

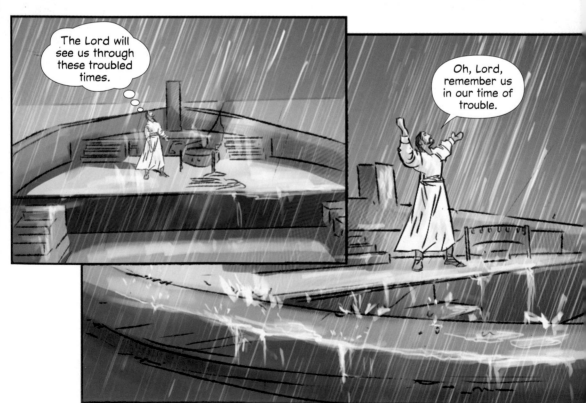

At last, the rains stopped.

We're saved! The rains have stopped! The flood is over!

It's over! Praise be! We've survived!

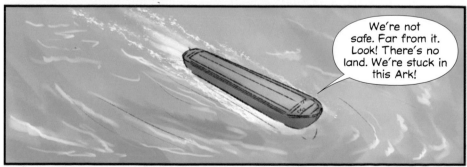

We're not safe. Far from it. Look! There's no land. We're stuck in this Ark!

All day long they watched but the birds did not return.

Then as the moon rose, the dove returned to the ark.

Look! She's back!

That means there was nowhere for her to land. How much longer can we last?

Good girl.

Have faith. Everything will be fine.

Noah sent the dove out again and again in search of land. He never gave up hope.

But then... one day...

Everybody! Come quickly!

...the dove returned with something special in its beak.

You good girl! I knew you wouldn't let us down. You've found land!

Not long afterwards, the waters began to drain from the land...

Land ahoy!

And God spoke unto Noah...

GO FORTH FROM THE ARK AND BRING WITH YOU EVERY LIVING THING THAT IS WITH YOU!

And Noah and his family left the ark with all the animals...

It was a brand new beginning for man and for the earth.

# THE FIRST FAMILY TREE

It can be hard keeping track of all the people in the Book of Genesis, so here is a family tree of Adam and Eve's children leading right up to the time of Noah and his sons.

# FURTHER TALES FROM GENESIS

In this book we have just looked at the first nine chapters of the book of Genesis. There are forty-one more chapters in Genesis, containing some of the greatest stories ever known to man. Here is just a brief summary of some of those stories...

## THE TOWER OF BABEL

In the years following the flood, the descendants of Noah's son Shem become numerous and powerful and the nations of the world combine together to build the tower of Babel that will reach into the heavens. The Lord sets an obstacle in their way by 'confusing their language, so that they cannot understand each other's speech.' Up until this time the people of the earth spoke only one language but from then on there were many different languages and mankind scattered all over the world.

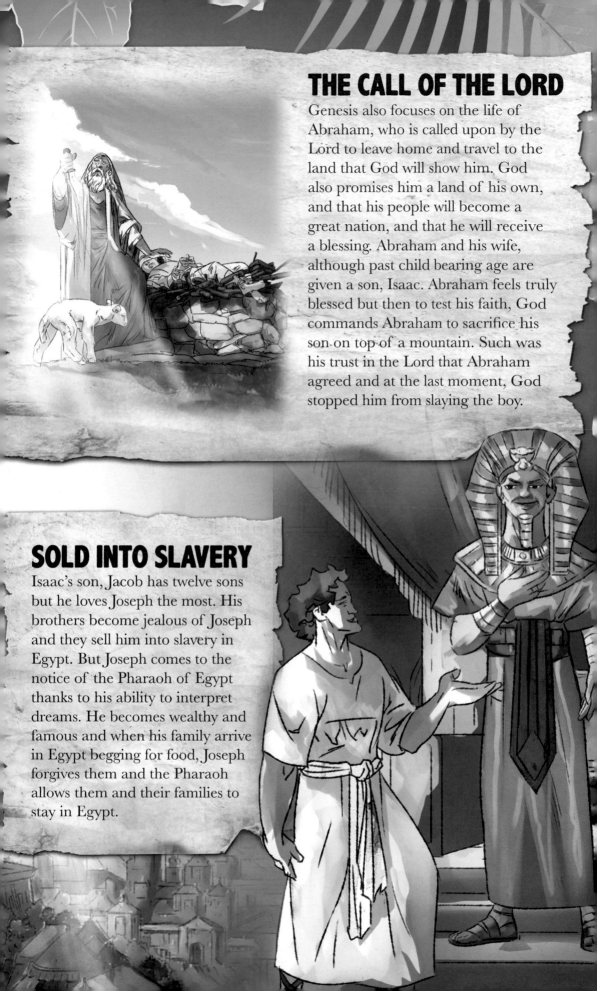

# THE CALL OF THE LORD

Genesis also focuses on the life of Abraham, who is called upon by the Lord to leave home and travel to the land that God will show him. God also promises him a land of his own, and that his people will become a great nation, and that he will receive a blessing. Abraham and his wife, although past child bearing age are given a son, Isaac. Abraham feels truly blessed but then to test his faith, God commands Abraham to sacrifice his son on top of a mountain. Such was his trust in the Lord that Abraham agreed and at the last moment, God stopped him from slaying the boy.

# SOLD INTO SLAVERY

Isaac's son, Jacob has twelve sons but he loves Joseph the most. His brothers become jealous of Joseph and they sell him into slavery in Egypt. But Joseph comes to the notice of the Pharaoh of Egypt thanks to his ability to interpret dreams. He becomes wealthy and famous and when his family arrive in Egypt begging for food, Joseph forgives them and the Pharaoh allows them and their families to stay in Egypt.

# THE GREAT FLOODS

The ancient world was full of stories very similar to that of Noah as told in the book of Genesis. Stories come from as far away as Chile and Australia, or Scandinavia and Nigeria. Almost every culture on Earth has its own tale of a great flood. Here are just a few of them.

## BY JUPITER!

The Romans believed that Jupiter was enraged by the evil ways of men and decided to destroy the world. At first he was going to send a great fire, but he was worried that the flames might destroy the realm of the gods too, so he decided to send a great flood to cleanse the earth. Deucalion and his wife, Pyrrha, built a boat and sailed to Mount Parnassus to escape the deluge. When Jupiter saw how good they were, he allowed them to live and called a halt to the flood.

## WATERY WALES

The Welsh people also have an ancient legend about a great flood. Dwyfan and Dwyfach built a boat and loaded it with pairs of every living creature before sailing away to the British Isles where they set about repopulating the world.

## THE EPIC TALE OF GILGAMESH

One of the oldest flood legends, and one that is strikingly similar to Noah's story, is found in the ancient Mesopotamian epic of Gilgamesh. Here, an old man, Utnapishtim, narrates to the hero Gilgamesh how the gods were once angry with humans and they sent a great flood to destroy them. One of the gods tells Utnapishtim to build a giant boat and bring his family, some baby animals and some seeds to be spared from the flood. After twelve days on water, the boat gets lodged on a mountain and Utnapishtim sends out, consecutively, a dove, a swallow, and finally a raven, which finds land.